ALSO BY TOM SEXTON

DARK CLOUD
IN ISABEL PASS

POEMS

TOM SEXTON

DARK CLOUD
IN ISABEL PASS

POEMS

IP

Loom Press
Amesbury, Massachusetts
2025

Dark Cloud in Isabel Pass
Copyright © 2025 by Tom Sexton

ISBN 978-0-931507-54-0
Printed in the United States of America
First edition

Design: Keith Finch
Author photograph: Kevin Harkins
Typeface: Adobe Garamond Pro
Printing: Versa Press, Illinois

Special thanks to Sharyn Sexton for her assistance in the preparation of this book.

Loom Press
15 Atlantic View, Amesbury, Massachusetts 01913
www.loompress.com
info@loompress.com

CONTENTS

AN EASTWARD LOOK

ON THE COAST OF MAINE

INTRODUCTION

Few writers blossom and flourish as late in life as Tom Sexton did. He published ten books after turning sixty in 2000 and another eight after seventy years old.

Tom Sexton labored on *Dark Clouds Over Isabel Pass* as he battled illness until his passing at age eighty-four. With his death in sight, he questioned his life's worth and wondered if he had been ambitious enough, if he should have tried harder to make more of a name for himself.

Although he published in some of the most esteemed journals on the continent (*Poetry, The Hudson Review, The Paris Review*) and received sterling reviews in publications from Ireland to New York to Alaska, Tom Sexton never achieved fame in the same league as Billy Collins, Mary Oliver, or Ted Kooser.

He never sought it.

He never attempted to mount an author platform. He had scant interest in developing a website. He and his wife Sharyn did not purchase their first personal computer until 1998. He never owned or learned to use a cell phone. In large part to limit his carbon footprint, he never took a flight in the last twenty-five years of his life.

Tom Sexton lived deliberately. He constructed a life that enabled him to focus on the things that mattered most to him: poetry, the natural world, and Sharyn, whom he met in Salem, Massachusetts, and married in 1968.

The Sextons lived together in the same modest one-story home on a residential street in West Anchorage for fifty-two years. Rooted in one place for so long, Tom Sexton developed a deep knowledge and intimate relationship with his chosen community. He tried to walk each day, often in the early morning before the sun cleared the Chugach Mountains east of the city. His sojourns might bring him past vast expanses of Cook Inlet, along Chester or Fish Creek, or into downtown Anchorage where he sometimes stopped for coffee or breakfast. On clear days, he'd scan the horizon for Denali, North America's tallest peak, a hundred miles to the north. He'd often walk along Westchester Lagoon, a man-made lake that hosted nesting waterfowl and Arctic terns in the summer and ice skaters on its frozen surface in winter.

Tom Sexton frequently stopped on his rambles to record an observation, an idea, or a poetic line on a piece of paper he carried in a pocket. Arriving home, he'd sit at his oversized Underwood typewriter or pull out a yellow legal pad or fire up his computer to develop a poem from his walking notes.

If all he'd ever done was publish the dozens of poems triggered during his Anchorage walks, Tom Sexton would rank as one of Alaska's, and the country's, greatest poets.

But his interests and travels ranged beyond his neighborhood.

In his seven plus decades in Alaska, Tom Sexton wrote about communities and natural and historic sites from Ketchikan to Fairbanks; from Delta Junction to Juneau; from Homer to Isabel Pass.

Some of Tom Sexton's finest poems rose from the ten years the Sextons owned the 12'x16' wood stove-heated cabin accessed by a mile-and-a-half hike from Hurricane Station House, 170 miles north of Anchorage. The cabin at the edge of a bog had a small west-facing window that framed a view of Denali. Tom and Sharyn got away to the cabin when they wanted to immerse themselves in the wonders of Alaska's Interior. They sold the cabin when noise from neighbors and visitors on snow machines became so pervasive that it destroyed the quiet and solitude the Sextons cherished.

After giving up the cabin, the Sextons drove through Canada every other year between 2002 and 2023 to winter at a house in Eastport, Maine, they bought with money from the cabin sale. They always left Maine in May to avoid Eastport's summer crowds and to get back to Anchorage's long early summer days.

Tom Sexton fell in love with Eastport where the downtown streets, brick buildings, and working-class residents reminded him of life in his hometown in Lowell, Massachusetts, a place he never got over, a place he returned to in his memories, dreams, and occasional visits. His recent book *Cummiskey Alley: New and Selected Lowell Poems* explores history, people, and places in that Massachusetts mill town where he was born and raised.

With the publication of *Dark Cloud in Isabel Pass*, Tom Sexton completes a singular poetic journey that spans the continent. His work reminds us to pay attention and question; to celebrate, laugh and wonder; to value, respect, and speak for all we love as we journey through this world.

Tom Sexton's legacy will live for generations.

—Mike McCormick, Eagle River, Alaska

NORTH

At Teslin Lake, Yukon Territory

When the camper van's sliding door slid open,
a couple wearing what I took to be
matching wool jackets and lederhosen
leaned out and asked, "Good place for wolves?"
They were Germans and rented the van in Vancouver.
A half-century ago, in a kind of grisly competition,
most highway lodges had a wolf pelt or two nailed to a wall.
Their glassy eyes didn't leave you for a moment.

That's what I was about to tell them. Lederhosen?
But their joy, the beatific glow on their faces,
caused me to point to a game trail leading to the lake
where decades ago, my wife saw her wolf.
It glanced her way then it was gone. It's the perfect
place, I said, but don't say a word, or step on a twig.

On the Yellowhead, Kandahar, Saskatchewan

I drove past the sign to Kandahar in a highway daze
before the name registered and I turned the car around.
There wasn't much to visit. The only person I met
said, "It was named by railroad executives for a
victory in Afghanistan during bug-eyed Victoria's reign."
No Empire for him. The first settlers were Icelandic,
drawn to Canada by the promise of land by the rails
and Big Quill Lake. He was collecting quills to sell
to calligraphers, which reminded him of a story
about the town's first postmaster, Thor Halldorson,
who taught the birds Icelandic by reciting the *Sagas*
to them spring after spring upon their return,
but he doubted Thor's coffin was made of quills.
It was Fall 2010. Kandahar was about to fall again.

Medicine Hat, Alberta

During the Great Depression, word spread
that Medicine Hat was a welcoming place
for families walking the railroad tracks,
for families whose lives had blown away.

They made pottery there, and the owners
of the factory allowed people to sleep
in the kilns at night while they cooled down.
One rule: the kilns were to be empty by dawn.
It was a small kindness if you think about it:
the kilns were empty, people needed sleep.
Rudyard Kipling, who once paid a visit
to Medicine Hat, would have hissed *Socialism*.
Small children, savoring the very last morsel
of warmth before they left, lingered by the door.

To the Poet Stanley Kunitz

1.

One morning your beloved Provincetown garden
will be beneath the waves
unless human nature somehow changes.
I imagine you'd say, "When we learn to love."
Like you, I was born in a Massachusetts
factory town. I now live in Alaska
where Uncle Sam sent me when I was eighteen.
I have pale blue iris from the Interior in my garden
and three darker shades from nearer the coast.
My favorite is a rare white with a ghost of blue.
I tell anyone who asks that it's the iris Wang Wei
climbed all night though freezing rain to see.

When the ground thaws, I'm going to plant a larch.
It's called hackmatack or tamarack in our neck
of the woods. I love that brick wall K
and how they drop their needles in November.
As you can see, I favor transplants from the wild.

2.

North of here, bodies buried millennia ago
are washing out of riverbanks, Native villages
moving to higher ground. We're all complicit;
still, peonies thrive here now. They're flown
to China just in time for summer weddings.
I imagine handlers opening the heavy doors
of cargo planes to reveal our *Monet of Peonies*.
I'm crankier day by day. Who curses peonies?
I'll soon be speaking only to the dead.
The radio said that with luck we'll be able to see
The Northern Lights around 2 a.m.
Have you seen them dancing from your garden?
They must reach Provincetown from time to time.

Trickster

It wasn't one of the ravens I see mornings
on the path beside my favorite stream.
Its large beak could have been a visor
like those knights wore on their helmets
to protect their eyes. It stopped strutting
to take my measure. "Wingless as an otter,
featherless as a stone," it chortled.
If it had lifted its beak, would I have been blinded?

Recollection

A half century ago, I held a crown made of
gold above the head of a soon-to-be bride
in the onion-domed church I glimpse
when the road curves toward the sea.
The groom was a colleague and then
a friend so I was asked to hold a crown.
"Don't let it touch her veil or the marriage
will fail," an elderly woman hissed in my ear.

Did my arms tremble even for a moment?
I can see the priest climbing the muddy path
to the church from the bride's ancestral village.
He's slipping back as he climbs, but he never
loses his balance, then he's leading us down,
our shoes knobby with mud, rain beginning to fall.

Driving Past the Road to Hurricane Station House

Long ago, I snowshoed to Hurricane Station
House in a canyon of snow carved by plows
with large steel wings attached to their fronts.
It was the winter of snow after snow after snow.
The next coal train was due from Healy
to the north in the morning, so I was taking
my time while composing these lines: "I could burst
from the snow like a flock of white-
tailed Ptarmigan and spiral toward the stars."
I was much younger then and full of hope.
It's New Year's Eve many decades later.
Hard rain's pounding on the hood of the car.
Not a trace of snow, not a hint of snow.

Creamer's Field Wildlife Refuge, Fairbanks

Beyond the fields planted with barley
for the cranes, a speck of boreal forest
with nature trails, wild strawberries, pale iris,
seasonal marsh crossed by boardwalks now
jumbled like pick-up-sticks thrown down
by a demented hand. The permafrost is melting
around me. Unnoticed, birch and aspen
move north, refugees with no other choice.
Summer solstice. The fields are already turning brown.

Wolf Moon Rising

Years ago, I saw a wolf digging in the almost
snowless marsh we could see from our cabin.

Its face was covered with porcupine quills.
It was skin and bones, almost a shadow.

Was it starving? I stood at the window
watching it dig. My wife was at the stove

heating stew we brought with us from town.
Light drained from the sky as I watched

so I put my binoculars down. We said little
while we ate. When we blew out the lamps

and went to bed, the cabin was still warm.
We slept but we did not dream that night.

Fall

I keep one eye on the mountains to the east
on my early morning walk this time of year

to see if the tundra below the tallest peaks
is beginning to turn red, the red of a salmon

spawning in a creek. I know it won't last.
Birch and aspen leaves will fall with a sigh

leaving behind a sky both deep and wide.
I've outlived almost all of those I've loved.

After My Wife's Surgery

Eating breakfast alone at the kitchen table
after another long night of little sleep
while my wife slept in the arms of Morpheus,
I notice the apples on the tree we planted
many years ago are turning yellow
with a scarlet halfmoon near the stem.
Every year, they fall to the ground still green.

When I slice one open its flesh is hard
and its small tear-shaped seeds are white
not the deep brown I hoped to find.
Disappointed, I put a few of the seeds aside
to show to her the moment she wakes.
"Look at these seeds, I'll say, "They're as white
as Sleeping Beauty's dress" Then I'll ask for a kiss.

Winter Thaw

Mist drifts over tangled blackberry canes
over saplings wind-hooped to the ground;

it drifts past a cup-shaped songbird's nest
that's anchored to an eye-level branch,

a nest made of beach grass and hair;
it climbs a tamarack's knotty vertebrae,

then like a magician's coin it disappears
leaving behind a voice that seems to say:

Once I was a vernal pool, once I was a glacier.
Step out of those winter weary bones and rise.

Matthew Henson
For Jack Reece

Henson felt a burning in his chest while he watched
Commander Peary lift the precious sextant
from its box so he could take the measurements
that would prove that they were first to the North Pole.
When at last Peary raised the Stars and Stripes,
Henson rushed forward and offered his hand,
but the Commander turned away from the hand
as if Henson were a ghost, another mirage:
a Black man standing beside him at the Pole.

Walking like a polar bear the way the Inuit
taught him to do, Henson led a brooding Peary
around leads in the always treacherous ice
and finally to their ship still locked in its grip.
When word finally reached the Explorer's Club,
in New York, those few who also wore the Arctic
like a scar whispered to each other, "Henson
led the way," then they raised a glass to him
before their silence buried poor Henson alive.

Recent discoveries suggest Henson didn't reach the Pole,
but he did father several Inuit children.

Transfiguration of Our Lord, Ninilchik

In memory of Suzie Fair

I held a crown of gold over the veiled head
of a young bride-to-be many years ago
in this small gold-domed church on a bluff.
When I caught sight of it today, my thoughts
turned to a darker scene, a good friend who
would drive down here from Anchorage
when her every thought became an anchor
and every other road led straight to Hell
or Hades. She was proud to be a scholar.
She'd climb the muddy path to the church
where the priest would be waiting to unlock
the door before *leaving her in God's hands
for as long as she needed.* Somehow, he
knew when it was time for him to return.

When she stepped outside, the mountains
and the blue-green inlet seemed to sing.
She mentioned this to me once, never again.
I imagine her and the priest making their way
down to the village, exchanging small talk,
laughing if one of them slipped, almost fell.
Years away from this place, surrounded by
brooding mountains, she took her own life.
Between white crosses, fireweed in bloom.

Winter Flute

The stream I walk beside every morning
is almost iced over, but for now
a dark flute of quickly flowing water
is playing music of its own composing.
A scruffy raven standing on the far bank
bows three times as if he's the conductor.
I expect him to fly away, but he doesn't, so
I manage a nod in his direction, move on.

SpaceX

After supper I pour a shot of Irish whiskey
and wait by the window for the moon to rise.
When it does, I raise my glass and say: "Elon
Musk and his investors have their eye on you
old friend. Your titanium ore perfumes their dreams.
He expects to launch a moonshot in the morning,"
then with a slight catch in my throat I recite
a poem that Matsuo Basho composed in its honor,
a poem about moonlight falling on a cottonfield.

Motionless as Stone

I was climbing toward a small alpine lake
at the head of a valley and daydreaming
of finding nagoonberries, those small ruby-
red fruit Tlingits call *neigoon, little jewel.*
My dreaming ended with the *thump, thump*
of helicopters coming from a nearby valley.
As I watched, two locust-brown copters
passed overhead. Were they about to be
deployed, I wondered as their *thump,*
thump, thump, thump slowly faded away.

I'd forgotten our military trains in these valleys,
places almost as mountainous as Afghanistan
where women harvesting their crops for winter
will cease moving, become motionless as stone,
when they hear the same *thump, thump, thump.*
Little changes, I thought. More than a century ago,
our navy shelled then burned Angoon, a Tlingit
village down the coast to teach them a lesson.
I knelt down on the tundra. I bowed my head.

Quaking Aspen

The chainsaws that cut down dead white spruce
all summer not far from this path

are silent. A grove of quaking aspen
is drinking in the early morning light

swaying as if in a trance.
I've read of trees talking to each other

through their spreading roots.
What good news this newfound light must be.

Tourists

We should all wake as tourists one morning,
our eyes wide open waiting for the day
to begin, strange coins in our pockets.
We'll set out to find an excellent coffee
and nod hello to all the smiling shopkeepers.
Oh, how do they make such wonderful bread?
We'll admire the trees, read every plaque
on every house and government building.
There's no need to hurry. Our ship will wait
in the blue-green harbor for our return.

Upper East Fork Cabin, Denali National Park

1.

Long after midnight, soft light, thin cloud,
when I arrived at the old cabin,
Adolph Murie's home while he studied
the East Fork wolves. I put my 1920's
Underwood Standard on the table
by the window. It seemed the fitting
thing to do that night. Perhaps the ghost
of one of his wolves will be drawn
to the window when it hears the keys.
I imagined it would move without fear
unlike the one I saw walking on the edge
of the park road with a tracking collar around
his scrawny neck. That night I dreamt
I met Saint Francis of Assisi and his sidekick
the Wolf of Gubbio on the side of the road.
The wolf had a large trap on one mangled foot,
a trap the kneeling saint was trying to pry open.

2.

When I woke at 5 a.m., snow
had turned the greening world white.
For much of the morning, I watched
bus after bus crawling along
the park's only road as it begins
its climb to Polychrome Pass
like caterpillars crawling along a branch.
I could see faces pressed against
window after window, tourists hoping
the clouds would lift, a wolf appear.
If, as a poet, I could grant them one wish
it would be for the clouds
to suddenly lift, a gray with
a pure black mask, the mirror image
of one of Murie's wolves, to appear
loping along a ridge followed by her pups.

Early Morning, Late Winter

The first light of the morning causes the top
floors of the Conoco and Mobil Oil buildings
to glow like jars of honey held to the light.
I'm sitting at the kitchen table drinking coffee.
When I go outside to look for the morning paper
my neighbor who works for Conoco is driving
her new Lexus slowly up the street. We wave.
To the west, clouds catch fire one by one.

Looking Toward Denali on Our Anniversary

The tallest mountain in the Alaska Range, Denali,
glows like a diamond in the early morning light.
It was more than fifty years ago when I first
saw its summit with my wife by my side.
Did it really levitate while we watched in awe?
Our wedding bands were too bright not to be
noticed, now no one gives them a glance,
not friends nor strangers. "Why would anyone
want to stand on its summit?" I asked.
A not-yet friend who was one of the first,
as he said, to conquer her in winter, laughed
when I asked before he looked at me with pity.
All around us the trees were turning golden.
"Perhaps," my wife said, "a need to look down."

Mergansers

A little after dawn, I met a woman
on the path beside the creek
where yesterday I saw a pair of mergansers.
She works at the commercial bakery up
the hill I'd just come down.
We've met before, even stopped to chat
 once or twice, mostly about the weather.

Without a word, we adjusted our masks
and moved to opposite sides of the path,
an odd pandemic dance
but not one to please the dancers.
When she reached the top of the hill,
she turned and waved just once,
a simple gesture, leaven for my weary heart.

Skater in Fog, 2021

"800 new virus
cases, 680
yesterday, 20
perhaps more,
fatalities."
Thick winter fog.

A ghostly figure
in a yellow
jacket
skating circles
around an island

is all I can see.
He or she
(not they)
appears
briefly like
a figure carved
from oak
on a carousel
from long ago.
I linger, call hello.

John Muir Goes Berry Picking

The Tlingit women who let him
come along carried large woven
baskets stained red and almost black
from the juice of salmon and other berries.
Beside them, Muir was a gangly spider.
They picked in silence watching him.
They sensed he preferred the trees to them.

Baskets overflowing, they led him down
a path to a small clearing where a single
wild apple tree stood, its small fruit
puckered like rowanberries. They left
a basket behind. Muir spread his coat.
This is where he would make his bed
far from the howls he heard the night
before. The stars overhead for his lamp.

John Muir and the Cranes

Wet to the bone. Muir woke before dawn
in the clearing now covered with mist
where, like Adam, he had fallen asleep
the night before beneath an apple tree.
He thought he saw a crane not far away
bending over the now empty berry basket
the Tlingit women left behind for his supper.
Its red forehead was bobbing up and down.
One eye seemed to be taking his measure.
When he reached the spot where it stood,
it wasn't there. In its place was a woman
with a small basket of berries and a bit of fish.
"You look like you've been flying all night
with the cranes," she said, then she disappeared.

Fairbanks on the Summer Solstice

It was around 3 a.m. during our first summer
in Alaska. We were on our way home from a bar
where I played eight-ball with a man from Point Hope
who emptied my wallet without breaking a smile.
I can still hear his parting shot, "You should visit
Point Hope some time because you sure look
like you could use more light, a lot more light.
In Point Hope the June light doesn't even blink."

My wife was at the wheel with her sunglasses on.
"More than a week's lunch money," she said.
"Didn't you notice no one wanted to take your place?"
A cloud of chalk dust seemed to float around his head.
He's a shaman I declared, an Eskimo shaman.
That's the reason why I didn't win a single game.

April in Ketchikan

Wind-driven rain was falling so hard
that walking was like wading upstream.
"It's a shower," the hotel clerk said
when he handed me their only umbrella.
"Rain's expected later this afternoon."
Perched on the hills above the main street,
the Victorian houses have bragging rights.
One with glowing shingles leaned toward
its darker neighbors as if to discuss the azaleas
tumbling down from every nook-and-cranny.
When a gust of wind turned my umbrella
inside out, water rained down my arms and neck,
filled my pockets and then my shoes.
The next strong gust bent the umbrella like a straw.
When I turned back toward the New York Hotel,
a teenager in a pickup truck going toward the mill
yelled, "Only fairies carry umbrellas in Ketchikan,"
then gunning his engine he left me in his wake.
A raven watching my progress seemed to find me
amusing before it opened its umbrella, flew away.

To a Ruffed Grouse Crossing a Road

A friend who certainly knows his birds
said that I could not have seen you
in the middle of that narrow road
winding through two mountain ranges.
"That's far beyond their range," he said.
"That was a ptarmigan not a ruffed grouse."

No ptarmigan has ever had that punk's spike
of feathers we saw when you brought us
to a screeching halt, then catching our breath
we saw your downy-vested chicks coming behind.
And here you are now strutting across this page
while our poor friend, sad to say, is in his grave.

North of Indian River

The first winter night we spent in the scribed cabin
we bought from a down-on-his-luck hunter,
a hunter who had killed and eaten all of Alaska's
Big Game animals, all of them except the musk ox.
It was next once he got to the bank with our check.
We stayed up most of the night watching light
fill the cabin. I still remember how the varnished
logs seemed to drink the light, glow from within.

I imagined the neighbors we planned to visit soon
on our vintage wooden snowshoes were reading
Thoreau or if not Henry David certainly Muir,
but the next morning the first neighbor we visited,
one of only two who ever spent the winter there,
was listening to talk-radio when we approached his cabin.
Drinking coffee, we soon learned that black helicopters
were watching his every move and they would be watching
ours as well. On our next visit we learned all about contrails.

But he knew the name of every plant in the marsh and woods
as well as the name of every bird that came to his feeder.
If he had moose meat for winter, it was from one hit by a train
while it was walking on the tracks to avoid deep snow.
His coffee grinder was an army surplus sock and hammer,
and you couldn't leave without having another cup.
His partner had a small trust fund, so they drove to town
once a month to get what they needed. He hated to do it.
From time to time, we'd hear his ancient ski-doo
that sounded like a washing machine full of nuts and bolts
coming up the long marsh to our cabin with a little gift,
perhaps a small jar of that year's mountain ash liqueur.

A Little Domestic Poem

Glancing at the white
hair in my lap after
she's done cutting it
then trimming my beard,
my wife smiles and says,
"finished" followed by a smirk,
a loving one.
"Finished" is barber-speak.

"Eyebrows are next," she
says clicking her scissors.
She knows how much
I've come to treasure them.
I protest a moment too late.
"I no longer look like an owl,"
I whimper. Untying her barber's
cape, she asks, "Stuffed or snowy?"

Beginning

I'm beginning to resemble a heron
when I walk, my hands behind

my slightly curved back, my head
tilted to one side.

I've developed a taste for raw fish.
I expect my arms will soon be wings

and my long thinning hair a crest.
This of course is a matter of faith.

Chulitna Butte at Twilight

An animal track crossing
the marsh below fills

with pale blue light
that flares briefly

like a match.
I've seen this before.

It fills me with wonder
as if the animal who

made it was made of light.
It could be a wolf

but most likely
it was a skin and bones

coyote, pads
phosphorescent from

minerals in the marsh;
blue-tinged Sirius

appears and I go down.

Solitude

I'm looking down a long marsh where even
the tallest brush has vanished under snow
and beyond the marsh to the Alaska Range
with peaks tall enough to rival the stars.

I've taken a leave of absence from the world.
There's enough firewood to last until May.
If I ever manage to finish this poem, I'll read
it to the ermine who lives under the cabin.

Three Days Before Christmas

A tree with two nests, once hidden,
still in its branches, one high,
one low,
the highest, a warbler's,
the other might be a wren's.
Sweet song must have mingled in June
when the light seemed endless,
when branch after branch wore green.

A Photograph of a Young W.S. Merwin

Far too handsome to be a mere mortal
when he was young and seeking fame—
look at that Olympian gaze, those curls—
the gods, long out of favor, long banished,
drifting like clouds on Mount Olympus,
decided to have a little sport by luring
him to a blighted pineapple plantation
in Hawaii that no human could ever revive.

It's true they enjoyed his early poems, but—
but behind that pretty face was tempered steel.
The blighted ground soon began to bloom.
Visitors arrived and praised him to the heavens.
Some even began to consider him a god.
Green with envy, they refuse to look down.

Seamus Murphy and the Otters

When Seamus Murphy, the Irish Terrier,
refused to follow his ball into a lagoon
where it landed, I waded out to fetch it.
That's when I spotted the river otters
swimming in my direction. Their hisses
sounding like an angry kettle on a hot stove.
I couldn't run so I told them the story
of St. Cuthbert and the otters who
warmed the saint's feet with their breath
when he staggered from the icy sea
after another long night of prayer. "They took
pity on him." I repeated this for emphasis.
They appeared to be thinking that over
before they swam away without another hiss.
It pays to be a bookish man I said to Seamus
before, ball in hand, I waded back to shore.

Kathleen's Pigeon, South Fairbanks

One of the New York Irish who came north
to work on the oil pipeline and never left,
she's still blond and steely-eyed,
tougher than nails except for her heart.
She's tossing bread to the neighborhood's
flock of feral pigeons while we chat.

Did I want some of her Irish soda bread,
the best west of the River Shannon,
its secret being carraway seeds?
She saves a bit for the pure black pigeon
with a little white at the tip of each wing.
I watch as it avoids the morning scrum
by standing slightly off to one side.
"Something almost saintly about her," Kathleen sighs.

Whimbrel

I watch a Korean Airline's plane,
robin's egg blue, celadon,

leave Anchorage International
and climb into a perfect sky,

Breathing the Blue
according to the internet,

Blue cocktails served in the bar.
Leonardo's dream of flight?

Behind the plane, a spreading contrail.
I've been scanning a tidal marsh

not far from the airport's edge
where a friend, a blue note

in his voice, said he might
have heard the piping of a whimbrel.

On a Winter Night

It's bitter cold tonight, not a cloud
or a breath of cloud in sight.
All the stars have their wet noses
pressed against heaven's window
according to a certain Norwegian poet.
Reason tells me there is no heaven
and no window to press a nose against.
If heaven does exist, why would the stars
be looking down? We cast so little light.

Picking Wild Strawberries Near Delta Junction

Here the mountains play second fiddle
to the fields about to be cut for hay.
The silty Tanana River, having shed
its skin of morning mist, flicks its tongue.
I'm walking the perimeter of a wide field
with my dog, Murphy, who thinks he's a pogo stick.
My coffee can is almost full of berries.
How could anyone think I lack ambition?

Green-Winged Teal

It's after supper, a good time for a walk
along the small stream near my house
where yesterday I saw a green-winged teal
followed by six chicks swimming upstream
in an unwavering line, a downy arrow.
I'll sit by the stream and do nothing.
That's what poets do, some poets anyway.
One time I saw not one but two rainbow rise.

Wilson's Warblers

Every year when the August air begins
to cool and people say, "Fall's in the air,"
they appear for a few days seldom more,
we're a brief stop on their journey south,
a sudden wisp of gold with a pitch-black cap
feeding on insects on our Persian lilac
we planted not far from our kitchen window.
Fewer now, not the spilled purse of years ago.

Sunday Morning

A saltwater marsh shaped like a ladle
filling with icy water at almost high tide,

sea smoke rising from its handle.
It's just after dawn,

soft light, my favorite time of day
when everything seems to be possible;

cattails bow their brown heads
like monks at their morning prayers.

I add hallelujah three times then fall silent.
Nearby a raven is practicing his sermon.

Raven on the Winter Solstice

It's as if he's put the light in a sack
as black as the feathers on his back

when he flew away a few minutes ago.
According to myth, he'll let it go

at dawn or he won't. This much is clear.
winter seems longer year after year.

It's the longest night, the shortest day.
A raven has taken the light away.

If he returns at dawn and opens his sack,
I'll praise every feather on his back.

I'll offer him bread with carraway seeds.
I'll praise his beak and his backward knees.

Fall Equinox

It's far too early for heavy snow,
but there it is on the mountains
now that the sky is beginning to lighten.

Not a single leaf is left on the trees.
They know the heaviness of snow
unlike the glaciers which welcome it.

I tell this to the marsh, to the black spruce
bent almost to the ground like old men
climbing through snow in a print by Hiroshige.

With Stars for Oars
For Joy

I've been watching a sliver of moon
rowing west over the Alaska Range
like a Viking longship with stars for oars.
I hope you're feeling well enough
to have seen it from your bedroom
if your English sky was clear last night.
Have we wasted our lives writing poems?
Send a few lines when you can, dear friend.

Meditation, August 2019

I'm sitting by the window reading Marcus Aurelius
that long ago philosopher stoic as the moon
in that twilight that is an Alaskan summer night.
I'm trying to calm my mind, to accept that life
is brief, that good men and bad men come and go.

Over the Chugach mountains, a few clouds like sheets
hung on a line to dry, and in the garden that will soon
begin to die, a summer squash lifts its golden trumpet.
A cool breeze from the north bends the grass with a sigh.
Fall will be brief, and the coming winter will be long.

Approaching my Eightieth Year

Mist is rising from the last of the snow that fell
last winter on the foothills behind the city
while I take my walk a little after dawn
by a stream fed by springs and melting snow.
That Greek philosopher, Heraclitus, was right:
You can't step in the same river twice.
I'm about to turn 80, and I'm contemplating
letting my hair grow longer, letting it flow.

Black Spruce

The foothills beyond the Chulitna River
still wear their heavy winter coats,

and stars still dance on the stream
where we draw our drinking water,

but the calendar says it's spring.
I'll believe it when the black spruce

in the marsh rise from the snow
shaking it from their shoulders

like women adjusting their shawls
looking around, drinking in the light.

While Reading Rolf Jacobsen

I notice the birch and aspen have put on
their yellow frocks. Did it happen overnight
while I was sleeping or looking somewhere else?
He must have seen much the same in Norway.

A man not far from here has gotten a pear tree
to bear fruit because summers are now longer
and much warmer. This must be good news,
but the hemlock and spruce are turning brown.

Belted Kingfishers

The appear every August and take up
residence on a snag beside a small creek
about the time the first salmon return.
They dine on sticklebacks it seems.
Their song's a rattle full of pebbles
and not the least appealing to my ear
unlike the swift whistle of their flight
that seems to make the creek forget to flow.

Approaching the Winter Solstice

It was cold enough by November
that we had to chop new ice
once a day or more from the hole
in the stream where we got our water,
then, hoods up, our fur ruffs white with
frozen breath, we bent to our task
like monks at a sacred well who knew
that before long the light would lengthen—
slowly at first, then with a rush, a flood.

A Morning Walk

Time's hourglass filling
with light
has slowed our step,
measured now
but not diminished.
We walk in silence
with no need to speak

of coastal mountains,
ermine-white,
of their long
procession curving west,
of how our breath,
like sea smoke,
mingles with the icy air.

Glacier

We stood on the deck of a ferry at dawn
fifty years back and felt the cold breath

of a glacier that was mirrored in the icy water.
Harbor seals disappeared as we approached.

When the air filled with the thunder of the glacier's
calving, we gripped the rail, the ferry shuddered.

Who could have imagined how easy it would be
to turn a glacier to mist, to make a glacier vanish?

Perogies and Cowboy Poets

Inside the small depot that last saw a train
decades ago, the local Ukrainian
Woman's Club was holding a perogi
supper according to a notice on the door
that read perogies and cowboy poets tonight.
"Don't miss it," a clerk at the hotel told us.
"They make the best perogies in Alberta."

Two cowboys sat at a wobbly old table
discussing Shakespeare and drinking beer
while we devoured our plate of perogies.
They wore bollo ties and pearl-buttoned shirts.
"No one will believe this," I whispered to my wife
before they began to read. When we finally
wobbled out all the stars were dancing in a line.

Walking by Cook Inlet with My Wife

She often pauses on our morning walk
to scan the silty inlet for belugas

small white whales native to this water
that number fewer decade after decade.

A massive container ship, stacked from end-
to-end rounds Point Possession.

Should I have wanted more?
What a waste of time that would have been.

AN EASTWARD
LOOK

The Ancient Chinese Poets

I'm sometimes asked why I admire them.
Is it because they liked their wine?

This is always said with a knowing smile.
I've never been able to hold my drink.

I'm not aware I'm on a spiritual quest
as a woman suggested after a reading.

I just enjoy wandering in their poems,
passing easily through gate after gate.

To Du Fu

While drinking tea and reading your poems:
Your moonlight on a patch of moss,
men marching a thousand *li* to the frontier
then returning as dust,
the sadness of drinking wine alone,
a sail about to disappear,
I decide to go for a walk with the dog;
otherwise, I'll never write another line.

Black Muzzle

After breakfast, I read the paper and perhaps
a few poems by one of my favorite Chinese poets,
brief poems that open and close like a scroll.
If it's cold, my wife makes me wear a scarf
when I go for my walk. I no longer complain.
Should I have tried to make a name for myself?
Tu Tung-Po composed a poem to his dog,
Black Muzzle, one cold morning centuries ago.

Through Slanting Rain

By a stream below an abandoned beaver dam,
one white iris about to open,

a rare circumpolar wanderer, almost a ghost.
Was this the iris those Tang Dynasty poets,

boney old men still capable of wonder,
climbed all night through slanting rain to see.

They'd have understood the madness of our time.
Dark cloud in Isabel Pass, bitter wind rising.

Adressing Li Yu While Drinking Wine Alone

I'd been 80 for less than a month
when I first read Li Yu's poem about
the racket a wandering monk made
knocking on a moonlit gate,
a poem written when he was also 80.
A fellow crank but what a poet I sighed,
then lifting my cup I said, "If an old man
knocks on your gate tonight, let him in."

To Chang Yüeh
660-730 C.E.

"When drunk every move I made was a dance.
Everything that came out of my mouth, a poem.
Songbirds fell silent so they could listen."
How envious I was when I read those lines.
After wandering from bar to bar, I've fallen
into a gutter, used a granite curb for my pillow.
Even the pigeons had somewhere better to be.
Unlike you, I have no pleasant memories of drink.
The moon was the color of bile when I woke.
Everything that came out of my mouth was a groan.

After Reading Hinton's Anthology of Classical Chinese Poetry

Near the end of another long cold May,
blossoms on the apple tree show

a hint of pink. They'll open white.
We were once the youngest couple

on our street. Now we're the oldest.
A friend about to fly to Paris says:

"Money is a kind of song, an aria."
No one has ever returned to Peach

Blossom Spring, I'm tempted to say.
Forty years back he was a socialist.

Once we drank cheap wine,
read poetry until the stars gave up.

Wang Wei

A dense haze over the Alaska Range
to the west of the long marsh

where I once imagined meeting Wang Wei
one long summer night years ago.

The night sky was far too bright
for the stars to be seen.

They say the haze is from factories in China.
I'm glad he's not by my side tonight.

Man on a Cloisonné Vase

When I was still a boy with two good
legs, the Emperor's men snatched me

from my parent's yard and sent me
to the distant frontier to fight.

An old man now, I sit unnoticed
by a small pond waiting for the tip

of my bamboo rod to quiver.
I'll catch a carp my wife will carry home.

My last living son is on the frontier now.
It's whispered that the barbarians

are more numerous than the stars.
Night after night, boots on the road:

Conscripts marching toward the frontier.
They must come home by another road.

ON THE COAST
OF MAINE

Apple Picker

He's *from away* as the locals like to say,
not Frost's imagined Yankee native to this place.
I recognized his rusted-out car by the side
of the road before I saw him, legs wide
for balance. His feet planted in early snow.
His pole high in the tree he stood below.
He seemed just another end-of-the-roader
at the end of his road, but my heart was cold.
I sat and watched him from my warm car,
my lights out, out of sight, but not too far.
I watched as his knees seemed to buckle
when he bent over to lift his bucket.
His long white hair trailing like a comet's tail
in the wind-driven rain just turning to hail.

7 Sea Street

The tides rise and the tides fall around the massive
pilings built for eternity below a building
where accountants wearing green eyeshades
shaped like the scales on the herring they recorded
in heavy leather ledgers year after year asked:
"How many workers will we need for the season?
How many cans will be needed this year?
How many seasonal workers? How many children?"
The roof is sagging or falling in.
Pigeons enter and leave through missing windows.

A's Dory

A neighbor, almost a friend, we chat briefly
or wave when he goes by on his bike
made from other bikes, discarded,
given, bartered, found. He's a fixture
at the local thrift store and has a good eye.
The dory was found filling with water
below a closed-up summer place.

He sanded it all winter, followed by coat
after coat of varnish. "All its trim is teak
and its oarlocks are made of copper."
Fishing from it, he could be mistaken for
a meditating buddha except for the hand
jigging for mackerel. I've heard talk of a trust
fund that grows fatter every time it's mentioned.

Fading
Eastport, Maine

Led by a tall man with a flowing white beard,
their Neptune holding a trident made of driftwood,
mourners filled the narrow street
while I watched, uninvited, from the sidewalk.
I half expected to see a coffin passing by.
Men and women walked shoulder to shoulder.
The house they came from is no longer there.

Their wide ruddy faces and ginger-red hair
suggested Scotland's outer isles, the Hebrides.
Most wore Carhartt's and tall rubber boots.
They must have been workers from the salmon pens.
One woman held a tape cassette playing "Born in the USA"
as they turned a corner, moved out of sight.
Springsteen's voice fading with every step they took.

Water Street

Back in Alaska, pandemic days, we noticed
new houses had replaced most of the old
tumbledown ones that had a good view.
You'll pay a premium if it touches cloud.
Where's the man who smoked a corncob pipe,
a doppelganger for Popeye the Sailor Man?
Grow up, I mumble. Time to face life:
Some do cocktail parties. Some collect cans.

A man, picture a hippie's son turned speculator,
stands in front of a new house that's stained
Nantucket Red and yells, "Where the hell
are they?" A crow gives a sympathetic caw.
"It's almost nine and garbage pickup starts at eight,"
he sputters, so I ask if he rang his Captain's Bell.

Snowman

Two lumps of coal,
not buttons for eyes,
for his nose a carrot;

where did his maker
find that jaunty
derby on his head?
His crow-black scarf
is stiff like tar is stiff;

and why is he facing
the North Atlantic
with its funereal wind
and pounding surf
far from any town?

Beyond where he
stands impassive,
gulls rise then fall
then rise then fall again.

Gravedigger, Eastport

He's about to dig a grave just deep enough to hold an urn
not that far from the stone of *Captain Lincoln*
Master of the Brig Islam swept overboard and drowned
Near Cape Hatteras. The city hires a backhoe for the others.

He'll lead you to the oldest or to the newest grave if asked.
He'll be laid off at the end of October when the ground begins
to harden, but for now he has a job to do. Herring gulls sweep
overhead like waves cresting again and again. He begins to dig.

Fiddlehead Ferns Near Fort Kent

When I asked a woman what she was picking by the road
a few miles from Fort Kent where we plan to spend
the night and have Acadian ployes for breakfast,
she showed me the top of a fern she'd just cut off
then she said, "If you're French it's the top of the Bishop's
Crozier, if you're not then it's the top of a fiddlehead fern.
No matter what you call it, it knows what it is."
As we drove off, my wife said "fiddlehead." I thought crozier.

Listening to the Red Sox by Passamaquoddy Bay

The road took a swing to the east
and suddenly we were face-to-face
with a full moon over islands in a bay
idyllic in the slivered autumn light.
An owl hooted not too far away.
In response to her "oohs and aahs,"
I was about to say, "It's as round as a
Spalding," or to show my wit:
"It's a lot closer here than it is out West,"
but I didn't swing, and I didn't miss.

At the Grave of Joshua Bradford (1763-1800)

Of all the Masonic symbols carved on worthy Joshua
Bradford's marble stone now worn by time,
the *Weeping Virgin* holds my eye:
the slight smile upon her lips, the ample flesh
upon her thighs, she seems a woman not a symbol.
Behind her on the stone *Father Time,*
his massive wings forever motionless,
his hourglass forever out of reach,
bends to almost touch the ringlets in her hair
beneath a dull *Masonic Blazing Star.*
Who could pass them by without a sigh?

Blueberry Shack

Driving at dusk along the coast of New Brunswick
looking for shorebirds in every cove and marsh,
I noticed a small blue shack close to the road
and at least a dozen cars parked in a field.
Women dressed the way they dressed for church
when I was a boy were balancing paper plates
as they made their way to a cluster of tables
where they could enjoy a slice of blueberry pie.
They must have driven out from Saint John
with its pulpy stench and oily sky.
A few were wearing their winter plumage
even though it was late September.
We were the last customers in line for the day.
The women who left the shack, arms still
dusted with pastry flour, rose into the air,
then disappeared like snow buntings over a field.

Pleasant Point

A postage stamp of land with a road
into Eastport slicing it in half, the *"Res,"*
Indian Days in the fall draw a few tourists
who might buy a sweetgrass basket,
but its winter now. A woman and a child
hitching. Not one car stops or slows.
"We've no room with the dog," I tell my wife.
They smile and wave as we try to avoid their eyes.

We've broken every promise ever made to them
since they fought on our side against the British.
In 1918, Private Moses Neptune, Passamaquoddy,
killed in France on the day before the Armistice,
was granted citizenship six years after his death.
When Robert Frost wrote this line, "The land
was ours before we were the land's," he lied.

Wolves

About a quarter century ago, in a town
once remembered for chicken blood
running down its streets before turning
the harbor red, a city official made it clear
when informed there was a plan
to reintroduce wolves to Maine that he
didn't want to see wolves at the end of the drive
when he opened the door to get the morning paper.

I imagine him opening that door
and spotting a wolf holding a suitcase
and waving to him from the end of the drive,
a wolf who was on his way to visit family
near *Rivière-du-Loup* up north in *Québec,*
but seeing the herds of tourists in town
decided to linger, perhaps settle down.

ABOUT THE AUTHOR

Tom Sexton (1940-2025) was born and grew up in Lowell, Massachusetts, along the Concord and Merrimack rivers. He graduated from public high school in 1958 and served in the U. S. Army for three years, part of the time in Alaska.

After military service he studied at Northern Essex Community College in Haverhill upriver from Lowell. There, he helped establish the school's literary journal called *Parnassus*, which has won awards and is still publishing poetry and prose. He enrolled at Salem State College (now Salem State University) in Salem, Massachusetts, earning a bachelor's degree in English in 1968.

He then returned to Alaska, earning a Master of Fine Arts degree at the University of Alaska, Fairbanks. On the faculty at the Anchorage campus (1970-1994), he taught English and creative writing and chaired the department. Tom was a founding editor of the highly regarded and nationally distributed *Alaska Quarterly Review*. In 1995, the Alaska State Council on the Arts appointed him to serve a term as Poet Laureate of the state. Tom lived in Anchorage with his wife, Sharyn.

He is the author of 17 other books of poetry including *Cummiskey Alley: New and Selected Lowell Poems, Li Bai Rides a Celestial Dolphin Home, A Ladder of Cranes, I Think Again of Those Ancient Chinese Poets,* and *For the Sake of the Light: New and Selected Poems.*